IT PROJECT MANAGEMENT—EXPLAINED

IT PROJECT MANAGEMENT—EXPLAINED

For Software Developers

KRISHNAN VASUDEVAN

PARTRIDGE
A Penguin Company

Partridge books may be ordered through booksellers or by contacting:

Partridge India
Phone: 000.800.10062.62

CONTENTS

PREFACE

Have you ever been bogged down and exasperated by the mire of activities to do under what often goes by the name of "Project Quality Process"? Ever wondered if those reports are even read and if all the data collected has any use and if it is anything more than just a mandate for process compliance? Have you ever discussed with friends on what your Project Manager might be busy with as you struggle for long hours to do the development work on the engagement?

I am sure you would have had atleast some of these normal questions that occur to every software professional at some point in the early part of their career. I too have had these questions arising in my mind and have wondered why someone would add more burden on me instead of allowing me to finish my work and go home at an earthly hour.

All the discussions I have had with my team-mates led me to the desire to produce a short write-up on this topic. I toyed with the idea for a long while and finally started to write in 2012. After a couple of starts and stops where I wrote furiously for a period and then kept it on hold, the write-up is ready for the first look.

In this write-up, I attempt to de-mystify what IT Project Management is, cut through the ominous-sounding terms, discuss the benefits and understand why clients and IT partners alike are keen on a systematic Project Management approach and most importantly, why a structured, objective and comprehensive Project Management approach will help you finish work Well *and* Fast and save you time to follow your hobbies and enjoy all the wonderful things in this world.

If you do not understand a certain concept, it is not your limitation but my oversight in explaining it clear enough. Please do bring it to my attention and I shall address it in my next revision.

I thank my friends and team-mates for their insightful discussions, my two junior team-mates who were kind enough to read the drafts multiple times and give their feedback and the organisations I have been associated with for providing me with the opportunities to observe, learn and practise. I thank my mentor, Elan, who has been like an elder brother to me and been a rock-solid support for me over the years. I also thank my family members who read the drafts and gave their suggestions on the flow of the contents.

1   IT—A GROWTH ENABLER

An organisation generates revenue by carrying out business. To achieve a steady and sustainable growth, it has to constantly improve and innovate all its operations. Such an approach will help increase productivity, boost revenue and reduce costs.

Information Technology (IT) has been a growth enabler for all businesses for the past three decades. In certain cases, IT has been the game-changer for business growth, such as Telecom, Currency and Commodity trading, Wealth Management etc. Consider a couple of fascinating facts—

❖ Daily currency trading is $5.3 Trillion and over 80% is reported to be pure speculative in nature. That means the currency exchange is not followed with an exchange of goods or any service rendered.

❖ About 70% of global stock market trading is done by high-speed algorithm-driven software programs that run on high-end computers. The trades are executed at speeds of milli-seconds, or even micro-seconds.

Neither of these would have been possible without harnessing the power of IT. Due to the remarkable range in its areas of application, we have witnessed a massive increase in global IT spending over the time, the estimate by end of 2013 is in excess of $3.7 Trillion.

Companies typically spend about 2-4% of their revenues on IT. This necessitates the presence of an ever-maturing IT wing that is headed by a Chief Information Officer (CIO). The IT wing defines the technology roadmap (what direction to take for future direction of technology), the selection of eligible Technology partners and the guidelines for division of work between in-house and outsourced. Of course, they work in close coordination with other divisions such as Information Security, Global Resourcing Group etc.

As with any division that is a cost centre and does not generate revenue, especially one that is a significant contributor to the overall cost, there is a constant focus on IT to improve efficiency and thus achieve more output with less cost. Since many of the existing IT systems were developed long ago to cater to specific functions, redundancy is rampant. So is the difficulty to maintain or enhance a system. To cite a real-life instance, a leading global Bank had no less than 4 systems to do Credit Risk monitoring, resulting in significant duplication of functions.

There is no quick way out of this, organisations all over the globe define medium-term and long-term goals to streamline their IT systems and to eliminate many of them, "Sunset" as some call it. These goals are converted into annual targets, each successful year taking the organisation one step closer to their goals. IT initiatives are conceptualised to progress towards these goals.

Being a profit centre, the onus of funding IT initiatives that will in turn help boost revenue or reduce costs, lies with the Business groups (also known as Line of Business, LOB) in an organisation. In a Global Bank, the typical LOBs would be Commercial Banking, Retail Banking, Wealth Management, Investment Banking etc The top Executives of the Business groups, who are accountable for the revenue and profits, they are the sponsors for the planned IT spending. In a large organisation that has multiple lines of business, each Business group is independently responsible for its profit and so bears the cost of IT spending for those initiatives that will benefit its business.

2 PLANNING FOR INITIATIVES

At the beginning of every financial year, the Business sponsors from each LOB set up working committees to arrive at a list of Business initiatives to be taken up for the year. The working committee includes representatives from Business and IT groups. Each initiative is then taken through a Cost-Benefit Analysis (CBA) exercise. Based on the proposed spending for the year, the working committee sets a threshold for the benefits and all initiatives that cross the threshold are taken up as possible candidates for the year. The IT components of these Business initiatives are taken up by the IT group to plan and execute, within the given budget.

Once in a while, a large Business initiative (Eg: Core banking implementation) is envisioned that is strategic in nature. That means, it has a significant impact on the company's medium-term and long-term goals. Such initiatives that are often IT-enabled Business transformations, are termed Programs. These programs run on multi-million $ budgets and span across years, ranging anywhere from 2-5 years and costing about 20-200$ Million. A program is led by a Program Manager. Each program is split into multiple projects and each project is run on a separate track, with a dedicated team comprising of Business and IT teams. This helps to sustain the focus and measure progress regularly. The Program Manager keeps a watch on the overall progress and provides periodic updates to the Business Sponsors on key progress-related indicators.

Where the IT Partner comes in

In the pre-India IT era, organisations depended to a large part on their own IT departments for their needs and at times, on local IT companies. Thanks to the currently prevalent outsourcing model that involves Indian and other Asian IT companies, overseas clients are now able to take advantage of the time zone difference and get more work done with a shorter turn-around time, that too at a cost-effective rate. Organisations that have a mature outsourcing model even stipulate targets to their IT wing on the minimum percentage of annual outsourcing. A large IT organisation usually has 3-4 preferred IT partners and it decides which partner to engage for an initiative.

Nowadays you will find three types of execution models of which the last two involve outsourcing—

1. Taken up entirely by the Organisation's in-house IT team, such as cases where the work is not yet structured enough to be outsourced or for engagements accessing sensitive Government data that prohibit involving an external vendor

2. Joint execution between the Organisation's IT team and the IT Partner. Most engagements fall under this category. The responsibilities are segregated between client's team and the IT Partner's team. In this model, the IT Manager from the Organisation is the client to the IT Partner. The decision on which IT Partner to engage, the cost and other terms and conditions of the engagement, the periodic payment are done by the IT Manager. It is not very uncommon where the in-house IT team finds itself competing with global IT Firms for a large IT program that a Business group has embarked on. This keeps the in-house IT team on its toes and ensures that it engages the best IT Firm to partner while bidding for the program.

3. Completely taken up by the IT Partner. Certain maintenance and production support engagements are executed in this manner. So are certain consulting engagements. In such cases, the IT Partner is engaged directly by the Business group, If the in-house IT team does not have the necessary expertise to undertake the planned engagement, this model becomes the only way forward. For eg: Creating a Technology roadmap for a large organisation to meet its 5-year goal, such as to create new ways of reaching rural customers, double its client base, create opportunities at rural outlets to sell new products based on client demographics etc

3   IT ORGANISATION STRUCTURE

In order to bring out the best value to their clients, IT organisations align their structure to the client's industry, such as Banking, Healthcare, Telecom etc and more specifically, to respective LOBs. As you know, each industry is called a Vertical. This helps the organisation to progressively utilise well the skills and business knowledge of the teams gained from multiple engagements. Thus, depending on the size, a Banking vertical division itself could have sub-verticals such as Commercial Banking, Investment Banking, Retail Banking etc. People who have gained a specific domain experience are re-deployed on engagements within their own domain, so that their learnings from previous engagements are leveraged.

Let me provide a simplistic overview of one type of organisation structure with a vertical Division. A vertical Division has dedicated client-facing and delivery teams for each client. The client-facing team is positioned near the client location. As expected, its primary role is to have a regular interaction with the client at all levels and build a good, working relationship. This team is involved in the discussions on all opportunities with the client and engages the delivery team as needed in pursuing them. The client-facing team is led by an Engagement Manager, assisted by Program Managers. The Engagement Manager holds the entire relationship with the client at onsite, each Program Manager is aligned to one or more LOBs.

The Delivery team is primarily located at offshore, headed by a Delivery Head. The Delivery Head will have some Delivery Managers (DM) or Group Project Managers (GPM) reporting to him/her and below them, Project Managers. A Group Project Manager, if associated with the engagement, has responsibilities similar to that of the Delivery Manager. In such a structure, there will be two or more GPMs reporting to the DM. The DM is the offshore counterpart of the Engagement Manager.

4 REQUEST FOR PROPOSAL (RFP)

Many key initiatives start off with a client floating a Request For Proposal (RFP) to a set of short-listed vendors, IT Firms with consulting expertise. The RFP would state the opportunity, the objectives and the timeframe within which a vendor must respond. The RFP is usually accompanied by a questionnaire that aims to gather information about the vendor's credentials and capabilities specific to this initiative. The vendor responds to the RFP by submitting a proposal document and the filled-up questionnaire.

A RFP is as much about stating the objectives as about identifying the right vendor by asking the right questions. As such, preparing a RFP for a strategic initiative itself can be a major exercise that needs significant analysis to get a clear picture of current state and a realistic expectation of future goals.

4.1   Initiative kick-off meeting

In the case of a multi-vendor RFP, there is a general practice to get all the vendor representatives together in a meeting and provide an overview of the initiative. This meeting is treated as the opportunity kick-off and provides the vendors a chance to familiarise themselves with the basic aspects of the initiative such as the business drivers, timelines and the various client stakeholders involved. However, as you might expect, not too many questions are asked during this meeting. Vendors reserve their questions for the next one-on-one meeting with the client manager, apparently not wanting to reveal their thoughts and information to their competitors!

I should mention here that in many cases the client might not float a RFP to multiple vendors; might just ask one, normally the predominant partner, to submit a proposal. This usually happens in the case of initiatives that are not very large or critical or in cases where the client is quite happy with the relationship with that partner. This makes good business sense because there are many occasions where the additional time and cost spent on a RFP process are an overkill for the initiative being undertaken.

4.2   Receiving the documents related to the initiative

The client IT manager hands over to the IT Partner's Onsite Manager (Engagement Manager or Program Manager), documents related to the RFP. These might include Project charter, Document of Understanding, Business Requirements Document (BRD) and System Appreciation Document (SAD), if the initiative is with respect to an existing system.

Project charter states the business objectives, system overview, scope and total estimated IT cost. It is prepared by the client IT manager and submitted to the working committee for review and approval. For both client IT and Business groups, this is the most important document in their decision-making process as the IT team will undertake an initiative only if the cost is approved by Business and the business group will approve it only if the cost-benefit analysis turns out a favourable finding.

A Document of Understanding is prepared as an annexure at times, to the Project charter. It serves to provide a next level of insight into what is needed from IT to meet the business objectives. It is useful for large or complex cases; by whetting out the technological needs better, it allows a more refined analysis of the proposed IT cost.

Business Requirements Document contains a structured outlay of all the business (functional) requirements needed in the new system. It is prepared by Business Analysts who are experts in that functional domain. They interact with the Business Users and elicit the requirements.

At times, the System Requirements Specifications (SRS) too is shared if it is completed. The SRS is a techno-functional document, it is a follow-up to the BRD and it is the translation of the business requirements to technical aspects. SRS is prepared by System Analysts who are good enough in the functional aspects to understand the requirements well and are experts in technology. Non-functional requirements such as performance, scalability (ability to support increased number of users without degradation in performance), accessibility (providing ability to use for people with special needs) etc are addressed in the SRS.

5   PROPOSAL SUBMISSION

On receiving the RFP, the process of proposal preparation commences. Unless specified, there is a standard turnaround time to submit a proposal that is agreed upon by the client and the IT Partner. You can take this to be around 10 business days.

These are the common steps leading to proposal submission—

5.1   Putting together the team

The IT Partner's Onsite Manager contacts the DM or GPM and gets offshore initiated on the RFP, who then puts the response team together. This team typically consists of the Proposal Anchor from Pre-sales team, the Proposal Owner (DM or GPM), the PM who will execute the engagement if it comes through and a few other team members from delivery to work on the estimation, documentation, follow-ups etc.

The team draws up a schedule for each activity, working backwards from the submission date. The first step is to analyse the documents from client so as to understand the requirements and other aspects of the initiative such as timelines, business criticality of the timelines (to know how critical the dependency on timelines are) and system features such as performance, usability, multi-language support, ease of operation by visually challenged etc. Such system features are commonly referred to as non-functional requirements. Many projects have come into grief, not because they did not adhere to the requirements but because they never asked and so never addressed completely the vital non-functional requirements that the users needed.

The team members come up with a list of questions, review them and arrive at a final list. The primary aim of this list is to get answers that will help the team in estimating the effort and in arriving at a solution to address the business objectives and propose the approach to implement the solution.

Since this list forms the first impression with the client, especially for a potential vendor, the team ensures that every available expertise is utilised to analyse the requirements. This helps in arriving at a set of questions that are precise and relevant. It is extremely important that the questions reveal a level of understanding of the initiative that might be expected from a top-quality IT Partner. If the questions of a vendor seem amateurish or irrelevant as compared to another, the battle is half lost.

5.2   Opportunity call

The opportunity call is where each vendor gets to discuss the initiative with the client after the documents have been reviewed. The date for each opportunity call is either announced by the client or is requested by each vendor. The questions are sent out to the client atleast a day ahead of the call. This allows the client manager enough time to get the answers from his team and as what invariably happens, plan to have some of his team members participate in the call.

The participants from the vendor's team will be the Onsite Engagement Manager, Proposal anchor, the Proposal Owner and the Project Manager. The PM drives the discussion, walking the client team through each question and noting down the response. Certain questions might lead to some action item for the client, which the PM will note so that it can be tracked. At the end of the call, the decision for a follow-up call is taken.

The countdown to proposal submission, as stated by the standard (or agreed upon) turnaround time, starts after this call.

5.3   Follow-up call

If a follow-up call is set up, it serves to clear up any lingering clarification and to get a status update on the action items. You should note that by this time the proposal preparation would be well underway, since not every section will have unanswered queries.

5.4   Proposal preparation

A typical proposal for a development initiative where the IT Partner has to quote a fixed price will be the outcome of the team's work through the following sections—

❖ Effort and Cost Estimation

❖ Scope

❖ Solution

❖ Execution approach

❖ Assumptions and Dependencies

❖ Critical Success Factors

❖ Roles and Responsibilities

❖ Risks

❖ Governance Model

❖ Communication protocol

❖ Contract model

❖ Financials

❖ Contract Termination terms and conditions

Let us look at each section a little more closely.

5.4.1 Effort and Cost Estimation

This is the starting point for a proposal preparation and an important step in ensuring that the engagement is executed smoothly, without unpleasant surprises. Based on the nature of the documents received from the client and the depth of information available about the requirements, the PM decides on the estimation methodology. The common ones are FP (Function Point) and SMC (Simple-Medium-Complex).

FP Estimation is where the requirements are broken down into individual functions and classified as one of the types of Transactions or Logical data storage. Each function or data element is further assigned a complexity (Simple, Medium, High). There is a pre-defined size ratio among a Simple, Medium and a Complex Function Point. This ratio is used to convert all Function Points into a common base, normally a Simple equivalent. Eg : If the ratio is 1:3:7, 2 Simple + 2 Medium + 1 Complex would be 15 Simple equivalent Function Points. Once the entire system is classified, the number of instances under each category is totalled up and thus the total size of the system in terms of Function Points is determined. Once the total size is estimated, it is multiplied by the productivity factor (estimated standard effort) for a Simple Function Point, as per the organization or industry standards, to arrive at the total effort estimate. The effort estimated will be inclusive of coding, code review, rework and unit testing.

FP Estimation helps to size the requirements independent of technology. Since it is an inventory of the business functions, it allows a clear verification of incremental cost for increase in scope. Any disproportionate increase in cost gets highlighted immediately.

In **SMC Estimation**, the whole proposed system is broken down into modules/components/screens. Then three levels of effort are defined along with the criteria—Simple, Medium and Complex. The effort required for each level is then stated, this effort will include coding, code review, rework and unit testing. Once the criteria for each level are established, each item is analysed and classified as Simple, Medium or Complex. In certain cases, if the spread of complexity of various components is too wide, we have introduced a fourth level, Very Complex. This is done to help us get a better-tuned estimate. With the classification complete, the total count in each level is taken and then translated into effort.

The advantage of defining the criteria for each level is that they can be reviewed by experts and fine-tuned to suit the requirement on hand. That then would adjust the estimates on its own.

When the technology to be used is known, SMC is a good technique as it provides a direct estimate on the planned work.

At times, requirements throw up technical challenges that might not be easy to estimate. In such instances, teams take the help of expertise from their technical groups that are set in place just to help the entire organization deliver technically challenging projects successfully. Such groups have experts in specific skills such J2EE, .NET and invest a lot of time and money in developing frameworks, tools, solutions etc.

The team working on the proposal, in conjunction with the Domain and technical groups, develops proofs of concept if required and completes the estimation exercise. A Proof Of Concept (POC), as you know, is a component developed to assess how a specific technical challenge can be overcome. It will not carry the usual frills of a regular system, but will focus only on the core technical concept that needs to be proved possible. Where conditions allow, I would encourage developing POCs liberally because a successfully proven concept helps to provide a better-tuned estimate, gives a higher confidence level to the team and the client and thus gives the team an edge over its competitors.

5.4.2 Scope

From a contractual perspective, this is the most important section. Any part left ambiguous could lead to a lot of confusion later with the client assuming certain items would be taken care of by the IT Partner, but the latter thinking otherwise. In engagements where timelines are critical from financial or regulatory compliance perspective, this could cause significant damage to the client and IT Partner.

Ok, enough of scary talk, let us see what this section entails.

Almost all clients have an internal IT team, so work on an initiative is usually done in collaboration between the client's IT team and the IT Partner's project team. A clear and precise scope states the inclusions and exclusions clearly from the IT Partner's perspective—list of components/ modules in scope, the list of activities in scope and those out of scope.

Common activities in scope are Requirements understanding, Design, Build (also called Coding) and Unit testing, Integration testing (for the components in scope) and providing support to the client's testing phases such as QA (Quality Assurance) and UAT (User Acceptance Testing). Activities commonly not in scope include Performance and Load testing (unless asked specifically by client), managing environments for various stages (Development, QA testing, UAT testing etc), user training, developing user manuals etc.

5.4.3 Solution

This section explains about the solution that is proposed to address the initiative. It normally depicts the current system and the proposed system. The solution has to be defined in such a manner that it is—

❖ **Relevant**
Is detailed enough such that it reflects a good understanding of the current system and carries relevance to the initiative at hand.

❖ **Precise**
The solution is outlined in a precise manner so that it is easily analysed and understood. Over-descriptive approach in presenting a solution can blur the message and cause flaws to escape undetected.

❖ **Efficient**
The solution is efficient in terms of performance, in the costs incurred, in the time taken to implement and causes the least disruption to the regular functioning of Business while it is being implemented.

❖ **Complete**

The proposed solution addresses all the tangible objectives targetted by the initiative. The usual challenge here is in understanding all the implicit (unstated) objectives that such an initiative entails and addressing them even without the client asking.

❖ **Scalable**

Is capable of supporting a larger scale of operations. Often, the projected scaling up of operations is checked with the client. This helps because there is a cost implication to provide "scaling up" to each stage. As you might have already inferred, this is not very different from how an infrastructure investment (eg: road widening) is planned keeping in view the projected increase in traffic over the next few years. You know it is too expensive and just not practical to plan for an investment that would support traffic for the next 50 years, because the cost would be enormous. On the other hand, planning for a scale-up to support 6 months' growth would be disastrous because it would be over-run in no time for all the cost and effort that went into the planning! (So those of us who think planning for a software solution is tough ought to try a hand at civil infrastructure!)

❖ **Maintainable**

Planned in a manner that future maintenance, which includes enhancements, is easy, takes minimal time to implement and is cost-effective. If adding a field to a screen requires $300K in expenditure and takes 9 months to develop, test and implement, then you know you have a problem at hand. Yes, I am exaggerating here but you get the idea!

5.4.4 Execution approach

This section elaborates on how the engagement will be executed. The success of this section lies in how well the envisaged/proposed solution is being translated into a practical execution approach. It contains the following parts—

❖ **Lifecycle phases of engagement**
The phases such as Requirements understanding, Design, Build and Unit test etc are listed. A diagram that depicts all the phases in a time-span mode serves to convey the duration as well as any overlap between two phases well. The activities done in each phases, the checks and measures done to ensure quality are described.

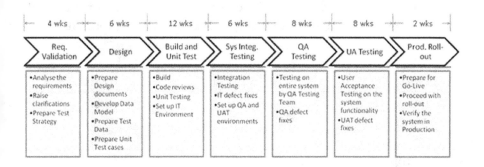

❖ **Entry and exit criteria for each phase**
Each phase will be dependent on certain inputs from the previous one, without which work will stall. For eg: Requirements understanding phase cannot proceed without the Requirements document being frozen. Similarly, Build cannot start without the design documents being finalised. Those dependencies from the previous phase are stated as the "Entry criteria" for a phase and the deliverables of a phase are stated as the "Exit criteria".

19

Thus one entry criterion for Requirements understanding phase could be "Business Requirements Document baselined". An exit criterion for that phase could be "All queries related to requirements clarified and closed". Similarly an entry criterion for Build phase could be "Design documents signed off"

❖ **Deliverables at each phase**
Deliverables to be submitted to the client during or at the end of each phase, such as Design documents, Data Model, intermediate code delivery (working code of a certain set of modules), Integration Test Plan and Test cases etc

❖ **Responsibilities of IT Partner and client team during each phase**
Key responsibilities of IT Partner and client team those are essential to help each phase proceed smoothly. For the Build phase, these are some of the activities that can be expected.

Activity	Responsibility
Coding	IT Partner
Provide Test data	Client
Internal Code review	IT Partner
Code drops at each milestone	IT Partner
Provide clarifications and resolve issues	Client
Independent Unit Testing	IT Partner
Fix all Testing Defects	IT Partner
Sign off deliverables	Client
Baseline source code	IT Partner
Set up environment for Integration Testing	Client

5.4.5   Assumptions and Dependencies

Listing assumptions help to clarify expectations of the IT Partner from the client on any aspect of the engagement. There would be assumptions that are specific to the engagement and some that are general. For eg: A specific assumption could be about the duration of client's QA/UAT testing during which the vendor's team will be providing support. A general assumption could be that all necessary software needed for the engagement and access to relevant systems would be provided by the client.

Certain assumptions might seem obvious but at times serious communication gaps can be avoided by stating them, especially if an IT Partner is working with that client for the first time.

Dependencies are what the IT Partner's team need from the client over the course of the engagement. Each dependency will have a "Due by" date associated and usually is in line with the lifecycle phases. Some common dependencies are System access, Baselined Requirements Documents, Availability of Client Business Analysts for clarifications, Baselined version of source code, Development environment (if coding is done on client systems), Masked test data, QA/UAT environment etc.

5.4.6   Critical Success Factors

All the factors that are critical to the success of this engagement are stated here. It helps to provide a good extract and thus avoid any oversight. Some of them are—Timely provision and support of development and test environments, adequate availability of time from Subject Matter Experts (SME), Infrastructure support team available during offshore working hours etc. For engagements where an existing licensed package is being replaced, a critical success factor would be the timing of the production roll-out of the new system, such that the existing package can be decommissioned before it is due for license renewal.

5.4.7 Roles and Responsibilities

The roles and responsibilities of those involved in the engagement, from both client and IT Partner teams, are outlined here. This would include the Client Senior Management, Client Project Manager, Business Analyst, IT Partner's Delivery Manager, Project Manager, Engagement Manager, Onsite Lead, Offshore Tech Lead and Developers.

Role	Key Responsibilities
Client Senior Management	• Overall responsibility for the engagement • Change management approval
IT Partner Engagement Manager	• Client Relationship Management • Account mining • Anchor project pre-engagement activities, contract management, initial planning with client • Conduct periodic reviews to assess health of engagement • Escalation management
Client Project Manager	• Client's Single Point of Contact (SPOC) for the engagement for decisions and operations • Conduct periodic status reviews on IT Partners activities and deliverables • Track adherence of Client team's responsibilities and timely reviews and sign-off of all deliverables • Act as the first level of escalation

IT Partner Delivery Manager	• Offshore delivery responsibility • People management—hiring right candidates, allocating them to engagements, facilitating trainings etc. • Client Relationship Management • Managing budgets • Drive Improvement and Innovation initiatives
IT Partner Onsite Lead	• Primary point of contact at onsite for Client delivery team for the engagement • Interact with offshore team to provide clarifications • Weekly status reporting to Client Project Manager • Discuss with client and establish agreed-upon set of standards and coding guidelines • Work on assigned deliverables • Review assigned deliverables and do a high-level check on all deliverables before submission to client
IT Partner Project Manager	• Responsible for Offshore's role in the engagement—On time delivery, quality standards of deliverables and executing the engagement within Budgetted cost • Status reporting • Ensure team's adherence to agreed-upon quality processes and practices • Ensure team's adherence to standards and coding guidelines

Client Business Analyst	• Define the requirements • Provide inputs and clarifications to delivery team on business requirements • Create the User Acceptance Test Plan and scenarios

5.4.8   Risks

Every engagement has certain attributes that are unique. Thus it naturally follows that there will be certain risks that are specific to that engagement. As much as the success of an engagement depends on accurate understanding of the client's requirements and translating them into an efficient technical solution, it is equally critical to assess the potential risks, come up with a suitable mitigation plan for each risk and track each risk periodically till it is no longer relevant. Further, a contingency plan too should be in place for each risk in case it gets impossible to mitigate a risk and it does materialise.

Some of the common risks are resignation of key team members, frequent change in requirements, development/testing environments not being ready on time, code getting overwritten due to multiple teams working on same version, test data not adequate enough to cover testing of all business rules as encountered in real situations, unreliable network connectivity, lack of environment support during off-hours (non-business hours) etc.

5.4.9   Governance Model

The structure of IT partner's delivery team is outlined here, along with the counterparts on the client side. Usually both reporting hierarchy and interaction are shown, this helps the client to know who can be reached in a situation. The section also outlines the escalation process between the client and the IT partner and point of contact at each level, status reporting procedure and format.

It is a standard practice to depict the structure as a diagram and then qualify it further as required. The diagram shown below is an example.

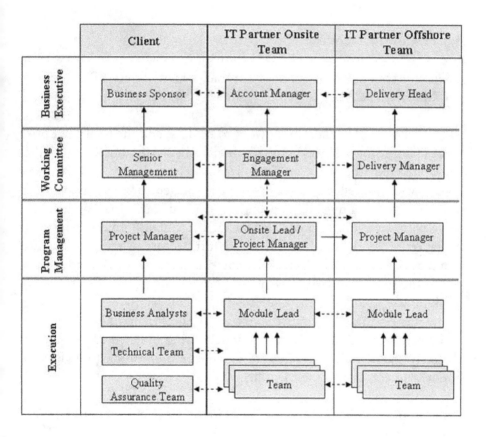

5.4.10 Communication protocol

The format of communication and reporting, frequency and the target group of stakeholders for each type of communication are mentioned. Typically, the planned reports consist of the Weekly Status Reports and the Monthly Status Reports.

5.4.11 Contract model

There are two common types of contract—Fixed Price (FP) and Time and Material (T&M).

FP model states the quantum of work to be done and the total fixed price to be charged for that work. In this model, the bottomline responsibility for completing the work on time lies entirely with the IT Partner, of course assuming all dependencies from the client are met as planned. You know this is a huge responsibility when you realise that estimates are done with high-level inputs. There have been many projects where the actual effort far exceeded the planned effort because of various unknown complexities and road-blocks that come up as you work through the requirements. The Project Manager gets all the blame for the team working late nights but the poor creature might hardly be at fault given the vagueness that surrounds the initial period of many initiatives! Yet, a competent Project Manager can definitely bring order in chaos quite in the early stages itself; that is where timely communication to higher-ups and when necessary, to the client helps.

If the scope of work changes over the course of the engagement, the client notifies the IT Partner who then estimates the change, which could be an increase or a reduction, and re-adjusts the price through a formal Change Request submission.

So how does FP model help? Why would any IT Partner choose to adopt a FP model to execute an engagement? Two reasons—it gives the company complete autonomy and control over how the engagement is to be executed and it boosts the company's credibility in the client's books because one of the points that clients hate is cost escalation. Many initiatives get dropped mid-way because of cost escalation. A FP engagement insulates the client from cost escalation even if the IT Partner did underestimate the requirements. Thus a reliable IT Partner who is keen to take up FP engagements will find the client willing to open up more initiatives for outsourcing.

A T&M model specifies the scope of activities to be done by a team and how many members are to be assigned to the team. In this model, the IT Partner provides a recommendation on how many team members should be included and what should the duration be but the client takes the decision on both. Consequently, it is a joint responsibility of the client and the IT Partner to ensure that the team is productive enough. In case the scope of work planned by the client changes, the client plans with the IT Partner to ramp-up or ramp-down the team correspondingly.

Such a model is more suitable for engagements where the scope of work is not very clear, is likely to be volatile or is expected to span out over a longer period. That is why you will see engagements on application maintenance, requirements gathering or consulting adopting this model. Such an arrangement gives the client greater flexibility in optimising the team based on how the work evolves.

The billing for the team in T&M is charged at actuals each month, meaning it is based on the team size and the actual number of hours/days worked in a month.

5.4.12 Financials

The billing milestones, categories of cost covered under the price and terms and conditions if any, are mentioned in this section. In FP engagements, the billing milestones relate closely to the delivery milestones, such as Completion of Design, Interim code drop, Completion of Build and Unit Test etc. The amount charged at a milestone is calculated in proportion to the planned effort from the previous milestone till this one.

In T&M engagements, the billing rate of each role at onsite as well as offshore (Project manager, Tech Lead, Senior Developer, Developer etc) is stated here and so is the estimated billing to be done each month.

5.4.13 Contract Termination terms and conditions

This part deals with the eventuality of contract termination, if such a situation arises. A well-written section ensures that both sides settle the termination amicably and keep the relationship intact. In a FP contract, it will specify what should the notice period be for termination, how the effort spent since the last billed milestone will be duly compensated and what will happen to the deliverables currently being worked on. For a T&M contract, this will specify the notice period for ramp-down of onsite team members and that for the offshore team members and the plan for the deliverables being worked on.

A word of caution—although extremely rare, there are chances that a IT Partner might come up against a client who is not keen to build a relationship, For such clients, the easiest excuse to terminate a contract would be to blame the quality of deliverables. That is why it is very imperative that the expected quality of deliverables is discussed and agreed upfront and timely sign-offs are obtained on the deliverables made at each stage. There was an engagement where the team worked long hours for weeks on end and delivered more than 50% of the deliverables but the IT Partner got paid only 15% of the contractual amount. We heard from certain sources that the contract was terminated because the client's IT team had undertaken the initiative without approval from Business and once they found the requirements were not aligning to Business, they blamed delivery and terminated the contract.

5.5　Proposal submission and walkthrough

After the exhaustive preparation and reviews at various levels, the proposal is ready for submission. The IT Partner's Engagement Manager or Program Manager submits it and schedules a meeting with the client to conduct a walk-through of the proposal. It is attended by the offshore Proposal Anchor, Proposal Owner and the Project Manager. The team articulates the solution and execution approach and answers all queries from the client. A well-conducted walk-through makes the difference and helps clinch the deal in a multi-bid scenario. So naturally, a lot of preparation goes into this with the team, which includes anticipating all possible queries and their responses, assigning specific responses to appropriate specialists and conducting a few dry runs.

6   START OF ENGAGEMENT

When the client reviews and approves the proposal that your company submitted, the fun starts!

The first step is to send the contract out and get it signed by authorised signatories on behalf of the client and your company. Once that is taken care of, the next crucial task is to put the team together to execute the engagement. Meanwhile, the routine activities of creating the project in the system, indenting for computers, software etc to be allocated to the project are done in parallel. As and when the team members are identified, they too are assigned to the project. Needless to say, the PM will be involved in the team short-listing process as his confidence in the team is very important.

Since there is a delay at times in getting the right team and for large opportunities, in getting the entire team, many companies start the core team identification process right after the opportunity discussions get underway. The PM marks those team members as "Blocked" with the help of the Resource Management Group (RMG) who, with their central view of allocations, help the Delivery unit in identifying the team members. The team is put through a refresher course of technical and domain training, specific to the upcoming engagement.

Meanwhile, the PM is introduced to the client Project Manager if it was not done earlier for some reason. They work together to take care of setup activities such as computer and desk facilities for those who would be travelling to client location (onsite) for this engagement and also to get the entire team the required access to systems.

With that, the team waits for Day 1!

7   PROJECT PLANNING AND MONITORING

Project management spans all three stages—Project Setup, Execution and Closure.

7.1   Project Setup

Project Setup covers all those activities that are to be done at the beginning of an engagement. The key ones are—

❖ Request for access to relevant systems if the work will be done on client's network or getting the necessary hardware and software to set up the environment on the IT Partner's network

❖ Identify all the stakeholders (everyone who has a direct interest in the engagement), setting up a communication process that will provide correct, complete, precise and timely status update to all stakeholders and establishing an escalation framework

❖ Decide on the team structure, the Module Leads and the CC (Configuration Controller)

❖ Re-estimate the effort if the original estimation was done by someone other than the PM or if more inputs have been provided since then that might allow for a better-tuned estimate

❖ Schedule a kick-off meeting with the client to go over the key aspects of the engagement once more, such as business objectives, timelines, scope, assumptions, dependencies, critical success factors, change management process and of course, risks.

As risks are the ones most difficult to handle due to their unpredictability and their ability to create havoc, let me spend a moment on risks. Theoretically, there can be scores of risks that can materialise during the course of an engagement. But not all of them cause serious trouble. In order to ensure that the important ones are not missed out, each risk is assessed for its probability and impact. They are rated on a numeric scale, usually 1-10. It is good to track those risks whose product of Probability and Impact (Probability x Impact) is greater than 5 as that indicates either those risks are fairly probable and can cause impact or that they might be low on probability but their impact is very high.

❖ Develop a project plan that will include the work breakdown structure, engagement goals, milestones etc

❖ Develop a Configuration Management (CM) Plan

❖ Assess the technical skills and business knowledge of team members as against what is required for the engagement and planning for their training

❖ Set up the development environment and document repository as per the Configuration Management Plan (CM Plan)

Project Setup is typically completed within two weeks of start of engagement.

7.2 Project Execution

During project execution, there are three key functions to perform—1) Project tracking and monitoring 2) Project reporting and 3) Reviews with senior management

7.2.1 Project tracking and monitoring

This is the most fundamental function. It forms the base on which everything else is built—timely correction, accurate reporting, predictable execution and effective management of client expectations.

What is Tracking and Monitoring?

Tracking and monitoring is a very simple and basic mechanism. Yet many teams struggle to implement it effectively because the practitioners don't either adopt it in a simple manner, do not educate their team members well enough and thus prevent them from contributing efficiently or do not track the right parameters.

Tracking is about the periodic capture of a set of data that will help in getting a clear view of the project's status. What data to track and monitor depends on what key aspects the stakeholders are interested in.

Let us see why the team's effective contribution is so critical. To know that better, we need to understand the elements of tracking and monitoring.

This is what the stakeholders of a project are primarily interested in—

a) Is the project on track to meet the stated objectives?

b) Is the project on schedule?

c) Is the project on track to meet expected quality?

d) Is the project on budget?

Monitoring relates to the periodic analysis of the data that is tracked in order to check if all those parameters are in control and more importantly, stable. Not very different from watching a boy ride a bicycle, the steadiness of the handle while he rides the bicycle will tell us if he is in control or if he is going to fall down soon!

Every bit of information collected from team members and analysed is aimed at getting an answer to the above questions. The more precise the answer, the better. So let us find out what is the information that helps get that clarity.

1) Effort

Once the schedule is drawn and work is allocated, the actual effort spent so far on each deliverable is tracked, in hours. This includes effort spent in—

a) Analysing or validating the requirements and raising clarifications

b) Designing the solution

c) Developing the deliverable

d) Reviewing it

e) Reworking to address the review comments

f) Testing, if applicable

g) Rework after testing

Change Management

Changes invariably crop up during the course of an engagement, be it in requirements or in design to address a certain technical challenge. These changes will have a cascading impact on the subsequent lifecycle stages. For instance, a new requirement will impact design, coding and testing. An increase in existing requirement or a new requirement will cause increase in the implementation effort. Most of the time, the schedule is re-adjusted in such a way that the overall timelines are not impacted. However, there are times when that is not possible. Every change is meticulously tracked and estimated. If the additional effort needed is quite low compared to the remaining effort, say less than 5%, it is usually absorbed into the existing timelines and cost. Else, a formal Change Request is raised stating the increase in scope, the effect on schedule if any, the increase in cost and the changes to future billing milestones to accommodate this cost.

A formal Change Management process is important for these reasons—

- ❖ It helps to provide adequate time to the team to complete their tasks. By adjusting the planned end date for the tasks that are impacted, there won't arise a perception that there was a slippage to the completion of that task

- ❖ The formal process provides the opportunity to ensure the changes are not missed—by enforcing entry in RTM, by updating Requirements, Design documents and Test cases before they are incorporated in code

❖ The extra cost incurred to be charged for the additional effort is reviewed and approved through a formal route

❖ Lack of a clear direction in the scope of the proposed system becomes evident if there are too many change requests. For a particular system enhancement, we faced 150 change requests and not surprisingly, the engagement was shelved on the first day of Build phase

2) Defects

These are comments reported during a deliverable's review and defects raised during testing. Details captured would be basic such as description of defect, deliverable it relates to, severity, cause of defect, who raised it and when, stage of lifecycle where this was raised (such as Design, Build, Integration testing etc) and additional comments/attachments to help understand the defect. The information to be captured while raising a defect should be such that it helps to analyse the data and look for trends

There are a couple of occurrences during testing phases that need a mention here—

❖ Testers, occasionally, raise defects that are not related to the stated requirements but are new requirements. This can happen if the testers do not stick to test cases strictly while testing.

❖ Even though the original defect is fixed, a defect gets re-opened at times if the tester encounters another defect during the re-test or if he wants to raise a new requirement. That is not the right approach, the correct way would be to close the original defect and raise a new one. Similarly, a new requirement should not be raised as a defect, either new or re-open. It should be raised through a Change Request.

Every re-opened defect raises a question on the efficiency of the delivery team and so, the Project Manager should take a close look at each. All valid re-opens should be analysed and corrective measures set in place to avoid them in future. Any defect that was re-opened without merit should be discussed with the client and re-classified accordingly.

3) Cost

When a project is started, an estimate of the total cost is drawn up so that the operating margins (profits) of the project may be assessed and tracked over the course of the engagement. An organisation has no reason to execute a project if it does not expect to get a profit, right?

The first two, effort and defects, are what the team members need to capture. Quite simple, wouldn't you agree? My own response would be Yes and No. If the activity categories are clearly defined and an efficient mechanism is provided to the team to capture effort spent for each activity, then it is simple. Similarly, if there is an effective way to raise multiple defects very quickly (by allowing commonly used fields as pre-filled) defect logging would be very quick and tracking, very effective.

Cost has two components—cost of team and cost of resources, hardware and software. At the time of estimation, both need to be factored in order to get a fairly accurate idea of the expected operating margin. Over the course of engagement, the actual costs are tracked and compared against the estimates. Some of the common reasons for costs to go up are—

a) Volume of work larger than estimated, thus needing more team members than planned

b) Experience mix of team is higher than estimated, meaning team has more experienced members than originally planned

c) Some onsite travel costs were not provided for

d) Some software or hardware costs were not provided for

How effort and defects data analysis provide an insight into current and projected quality aspects and also highlight or even predict possible areas of concern merits a dedicated section, Quantitative or Metrics-based Project Management.

Quantitative Project Management (QPM)

There are excellent books on QPM, I will just stick to the introduction and its purpose as an overview.

QPM refers to the practice of doing project management using measurable and comparable information. For eg : Effort variance in hours, review effectiveness in %, defect injection and detection rate as ratios, Cost of Quality etc.

Why is QPM needed?

Unless it is a very small team, a PM will find it overwhelming to look into all deliverables in depth and then assess the project's health. I have heard of a Core B anking Implementation Program attempted by a Global Bank, in partnership with a Global IT Partner, that was aborted after spending about $100 Million. What made it worse was that it need not have cost anywhere close to $100 Million to find out the Core Banking package being implemented would not address certain fundamental business processes.

QPM provides with mechanisms and indicators where a PM can quickly narrow down areas of higher concern and do a deeper analysis. When used effectively, QPM saves a significant amount of time for a PM. Use the spare time to watch cricket, read a book or go outdoors and enjoy nature!

I shall use a simple example to explain how gathering data and analysing them help in easy and yet accurate decision-making—

A Stock market Analyst has to assess four companies in Manufacturing sector and recommend one to his investors. He has picked up three pieces of information to start his analysis and see if he can do a quick elimination. Have a glimpse at the data he has compiled—

Company Name	No. of Employees	Debt-Equity Ratio	Rev. share of largest client A/c
ABC Industries Ltd	85,000	1.75	5%
KLM Engineering Ltd	1,50,000	8.50	3%
XYZ Machines Ltd	2,85,000	2.45	45%
DH Automations Ltd	3,75,000	2,25	6%

A note on the 2nd and 3rd parameters—Debt-Equity Ratio is the ratio of the company's debts (loans) to the total value of equity shares issued. Revenue share of largest client A/c reflects the revenue from the company's largest account as compared to the company's total revenue.

On analysing each parameter, this is what the analyst finds out—

1) No. of Employees
   He realises this was a wrong parameter to pick up for analysis. It does not reveal anything about the health or future prospects of the companies. So he decides to drop it.

2) Debt-Equity Ratio

   The ratios of ABC Industries, XYZ Machines and DH Automations seem fine but KLM Engineering seems to have taken excessively heavy loans. That will significantly hamper their expansion plans because they will not be able to take any more loans to fund their expansion. They will be forced to issue more equity shares to generate additional funding, which is the most expensive form of funding. That information helps the analyst eliminate KLM Engineering.

3) Revenue share of largest client A/c

   The revenue share of the largest client of XYZ Machines is 45% of the company's total revenues. That shows the client base of the company is not widespread. If the relationship with that client sours or if that client suffers a financial difficulty and puts its investments on hold, XYZ Machines will suffer a serious blow to its overall revenue. The analyst identifies this company as risky and eliminates it from his list.

By comparing these publicly available information, the analyst was immediately able to eliminate two of the four companies. Now he can use his time and energy to do a deeper analysis of the other two. If he had not gathered relevant information to do a first-level analysis, imagine how many months he would have wasted looking into the affairs of KLM Engineering and XYZ Machines before realising they should not be considered. This is the power of metrics and its use in QPM.

Let me list some of the essential indicators that aid a PM—

1) Effort variance

The variance between estimated effort and actual effort raises a couple of possibilities—

❖ There is a need for re-estimation

❖ Certain team members are struggling to meet the timelines, they need assistance

2) Effort spent on reviews/testing

❖ Check if review/testing effort is being spent as efficiently as estimated or if there is an issue with work planning/scheduling.

❖ Ratio of Review/testing effort to development effort
A low ratio indicates too little time spent on reviews/testing. A high ratio indicates possible time wasted. To proof-read one page of a book, about 15-20 minutes should be sufficient. Asking someone to proof-read for 3 hours is not going to help catch more mistakes from that page, it would be just a complete waste of time.

❖ Ratio of number of review comments/test defects to review/testing effort
A low ratio indicates to possible inefficiency, that the reviewers/testers have raised too few comments for the time spent. A high ratio could indicate poor quality

The analysis of effectiveness is more relevant for reviews though I have found it useful for testing as well when it comes to random testing. There was one instance where a project was in trouble after going live amd I was asked to help out. I put a testing team together and by end of first day, the 4-member team had raised 95 defects. Not bad I thought. Yet I asked for the report and checked on the number of defects raised by each person and guess what, I found that one tester had logged just 5 defects! So the remaining three testers had logged 90! I spoke to the Test lead and found that this tester had joined the team late and after getting a crash course on the system, had done only about an hour's testing. That seemed to be a satisfactory explanation for the low count. This approach is an example of how metrics used in the right way can help a PM identify an area of concern quickly and do a deeper analysis. This is also a great example to highlight that a metric is indicative but not conclusive. In the numerous sessions that I have conducted, this is one example that participants seemed to appreciate the most!

3) Defect Injection and detection rate

Based on skill level of team and complexity of work, an expected rate of defects being injected and detected in each phase are estimated. It is a good practice to track this regularly and check for any variance; a high rate needs a look into quality and a low rate, into testing efficiency.

To summarise the above points, the key is to check two aspects—first if enough effort is being spent on quality assurance activities and second, if they are detecting enough defects. A deviation on higher side would indicate a concern with quality of developing/coding, a deviation on lower side might point to a concern on quality of the checks. After all, it is unlikely that teams spring out unbelievably high quality of code. Unlikely but possible!

4) Root Cause Analysis (RCA)

Based on metrics collected, the PM and Team Leads conduct periodic Root Cause Analysis on the key issues/defects and arrive at appropriate improvement measures to prevent or reduce similar issues in future. A common tool used to carry out RCA effectively is a Fish bone diagram. It helps to diagrammatically list all causes and break them down to multiple levels, so that the key root causes are identified. Once identified, it is easier to find a solution. Since RCA is a time-consuming activity, it is done only on critical and major issues.

An example of a Fish bone diagram is shown below.

The "Effect" is High no. of critical defects. The top-level possible causes are Skills, Quality Process, Communication and Requirements. Each possible cause is then broken down to next level and a 3rd level if required. Once done, they are analysed and the key ones identified.

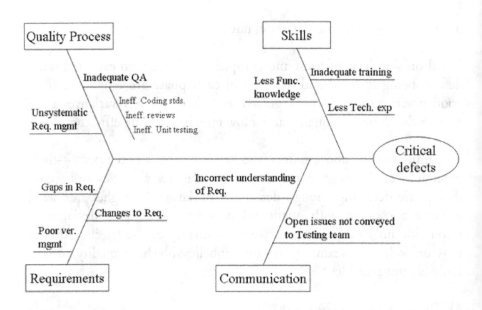

7.2.2   Project Reporting

Project reporting is primarily about informing all stakeholders about the status of project. The details to be reported and the frequency of reporting are planned as part of setup and done accordingly. The status report includes—

❖ Current phase of engagement

❖ Health indicator—Green, Amber or Red (Or 'On track', 'Risk of Delay', 'Delayed' or some variation of above)

❖ List of current deliverables, their timelines, % completion, status etc

❖ Key issues/dependencies/constraints

❖ Key risks

❖ Action plan and status of each

Reporting is done every week through status reports and then once in a month through milestone reports. For fixed price projects, the report is generated at the end of each milestone. In milestone reports, findings from metrics analysis are included.

Status reporting depends on the current lifecycle stage of an engagement as well. For instance, during Testing phase (SIT/UAT), everyone would be interested to know what is the count of open defects, how many were fixed by the team and what was the re-open rate of defects. So the status report gets fine-tuned to meet the needs at that stage.

The Weekly Status Report (WSR) is the first point of update to all stakeholders on the week's progress. If used well, this report can be very useful in bringing attention on all aspects that can potentially affect the engagement. For that, the PM should list critical issues, risks, concerns, dependencies along with a mention of when each is/was due and who is responsible. By doing this, if a deliverable is at risk of delay due to some unmet dependency, the question is asked to the right person. The WSR will also report the progress on the deliverables worked on during the week and if there were any delays, along with reasons. The key is in tracking the quantum of the delay (such as downtime of network) and reporting the consequent loss in productivity.

I have found it a good practice to provide a Summary or Key updates section at the top of WSR, it helps to bring attention immediately.

A vital point to note on the WSR is that it should be used only to consolidate and report information that has already been discussed with the respective teams. It should not be used as a tool to report for the first time, a risk or a concern. The stakeholders would expect that the PM would raise any point that is of importance with the respective team immediately and not wait till the week is up.

7.2.3 Senior management reviews

A periodic review of the engagement is conducted by Senior management, usually every month or quarter depending on criticality, duration and phase of engagement. The focus is on—

- ❖ Basic metrics—Schedule, effort, quality and budget

- ❖ Risks and backup planning

- ❖ Client escalations/appreciations

- ❖ People issues

- ❖ Action plan

This forum is ideal for a PM to bring all internal issues to the attention of senior management and get the necessary support for project execution.

7.3 Project Closure

On completion of an engagement, the project closure task is initiated. The objectives of closure are—

a) Collate learnings and best practices. Some of the common areas around which the learnings revolve are—Design considerations to handle massive volumes of data, optimising the Cost of Quality, planning around SIT and QA phases to make their coverage better

b) Collate reusable components (like code snippets, helper classes, framework etc) and reusable artifacts (like Book of knowledge, checklists, estimation methodology, innovative execution approach etc)

c) Derive the project metrics—productivity, effort, In-process defects and delivered defects, schedule deviation

Outputs from the first two objectives go into the organisation's Knowledge Repository so that anyone starting off a similar engagement can benefit from the experience. The metrics data goes to Quality Department's Capability Baseline and helps to refine the overall baseline on productivity, effort and schedule deviation and defect rate. The refined baseline helps to set a more realistic benchmark for future engagements.

8 DELIVERABLE VERIFICATION AND SIGN-OFF

The formal verification of deliverables happens through the User Acceptance Testing (UAT) phase. UAT is scheduled after System Integration Testing (SIT) phase and is planned such that it allows atleast 3 cycles of functional testing of the entire system.

UAT is done by a select group of end users, representative of the various roles that would be required to perform the entire gamut of functions once the system is implemented.

In the real world, clients do not wait for UAT to take a first look at the system. It is in the interest of both parties that the Subject Matter Experts of the client get an early glimpse of the system so that any critical issues are quickly addressed and the overall confidence level is high.

The success of UAT lies in the focussed rigour during the entire cycle and in a close communication among all the stakeholders. The project I cited earlier suffered after production release because when the UAT testers got tired of testing after raising over 200 defects and brace yourself, decided to go ahead with the implementation instead of sending it back for repairs!

9 PRODUCTION ROLL-OUT AND WARRANTY SUPPORT

9.1 Production roll-out

Preparations for roll-out to production environment are given final touches once UAT is successfully cleared. The Release Manager gets the UAT-approved version of the system deployed in the production environment. This is generally done at the start of a weekend and once the Release Manager gives the go-ahead, the various IT teams runs through their respective roll-out checklists. The entire roll-out exercise is controlled and directed by the client Project Manager. The client Project Manager assesses the outcome of the roll-out and if satisfied, gives the green signal to "Go Live". Meaning, the system can be opened up to the users.

In many cases, the system is rolled out in phases, adding a set of users or a certain Line of Business in each phase. While this minimises a risk to normal working if the new system fails for some reason, issues of login, performance, user workstation incompatibility etc, it does necessitate additional effort in terms of managing the data between the new system and the old till to the switch-over to the new one is complete.

It is a common practice to keep the old system ready for the first few days as a contingency measure in case the new system fails and users have to be continued on the old one. This, of course, will not be possible in cases where IT transformation is being carried out as part of business process reengineering (Business Transformation). As you have understood correctly, that is because the business processes would have been revamped and the old system will no longer be able to support the new business processes.

9.2 Warranty support

Like any regular product, a software release too carries a certain warranty period during which critical or high defects reported by users would be fixed by the IT Partner free of cost. The normal duration is about 3 months from production roll-out, which is plenty for an active system.

A sign-off note

This brings to a conclusion our discussion on Project Management, an insight into how it is planned and practised and how it benefits all of us. It will give me immense happiness to know that you find it useful, helps you do your work well and leaves you with more personal time to enjoy what you wish!